YOU ARE amazing

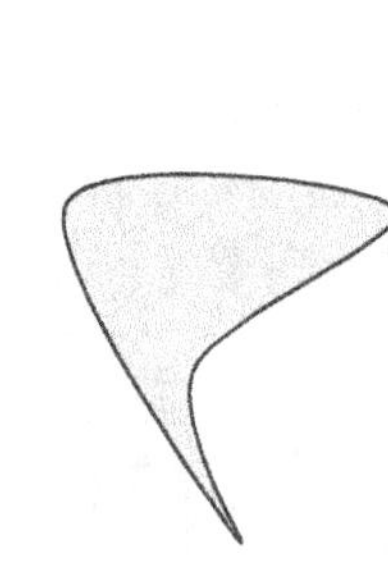

Seeing various colors can evoke emotion in us due to connections with real-life experience as well as how we feel a color is interpreted. While some colors are bright or dark by nature, others are muted or paler in comparison, allowing for drastically different interpretations. When you think about coloring pages in this way, you open up a world of experimentation where different sets of colors used on the same coloring page pattern can evoke different emotions. When you combine that knowledge with the proven fact that coloring is proven to help you feel better and more relaxed, you have a winning product combination. This book is full of inspiring phrases and quotes that you can color. This book contains different styles with inspirational phrases in several different styles. Patterns consist of 3 different sets of styles, phrases ranging from single words to long quotes - all inspirational and intended to help coloring to work with their emotions. In addition to this, the book also provides you with a set of great coloring pages without written phrases.

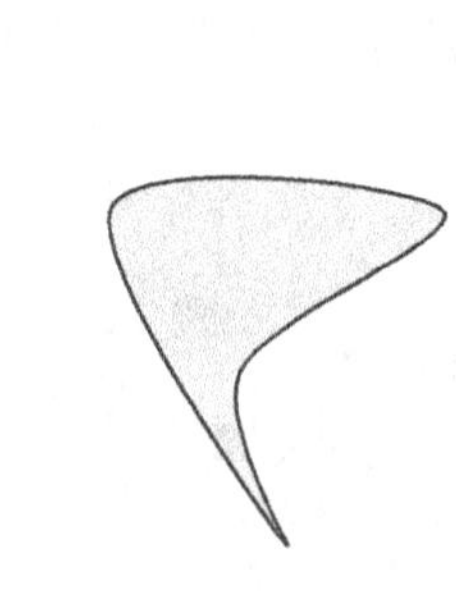

I AM
LIMITLESS

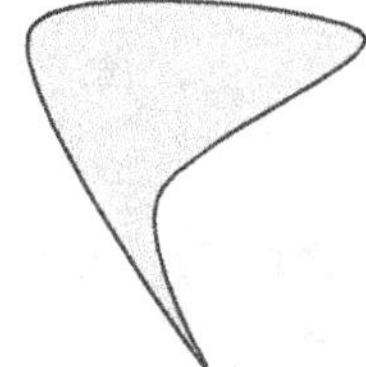

BEAUTY

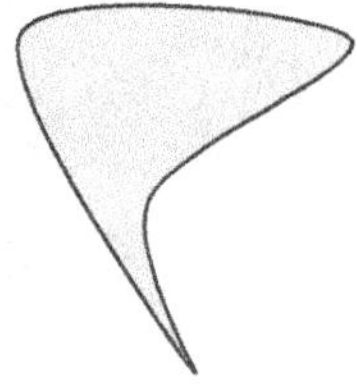

Reach for your Dreams.
The Universe will Rise to meet them.

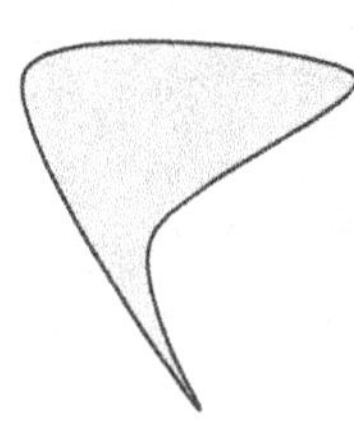

LOVE

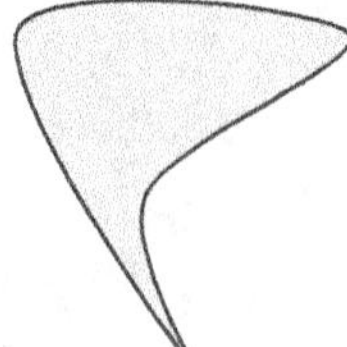

Remember, YOU teach people how to treat you.

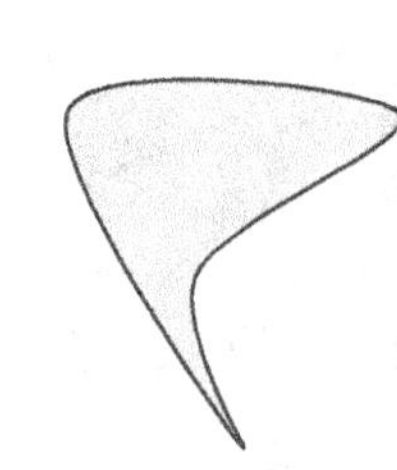

Reach for your Dreams.
The Universe will Rise to meet them.

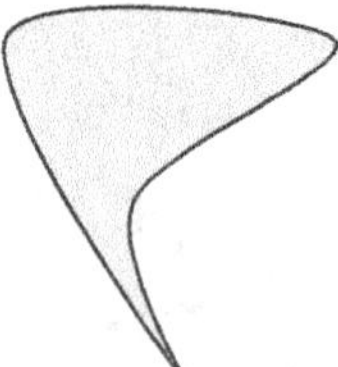

TRUST

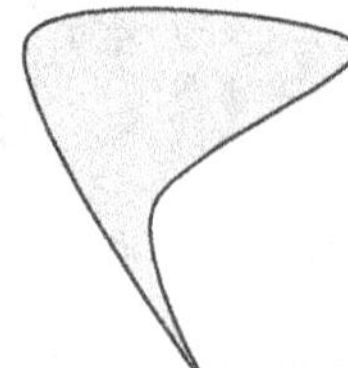

"Hard work keeps the wrinkles out of the mind and spirit."

— Helena Rubinstein.

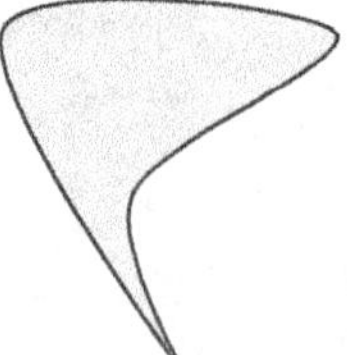

Do What Makes Your Soul Shine

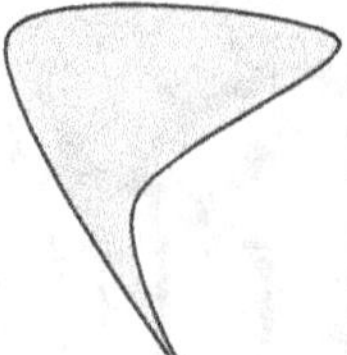

Dream It.
Wish It.
Do It.

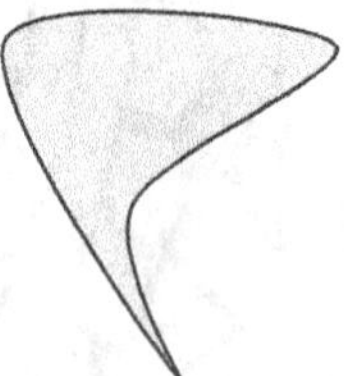

Sometimes
We're Tested
Not To Show
Our
Weaknesses,
But To
Discover Our
Strengths

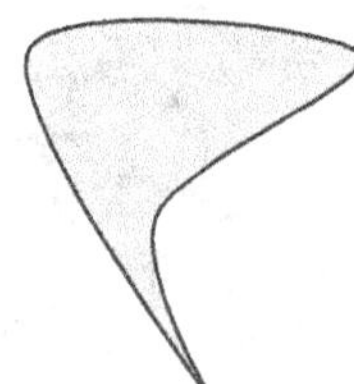

"Believe You Can
And You're
Halfway There."
Theodore
Roosevelt

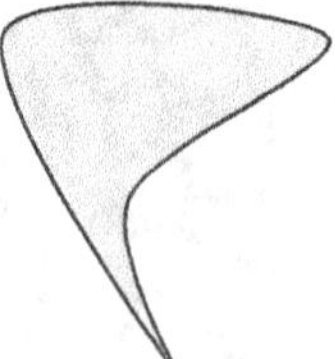

Do Something
Today That
Your Future
Self Will
Thank You
For

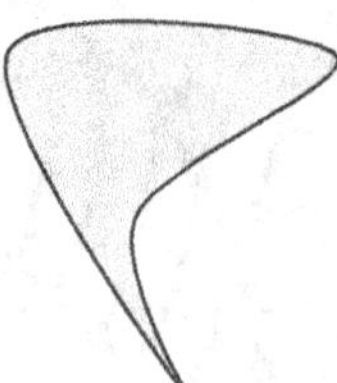

Do
Something
Today That
Your Future
Self Will
Thank You
For

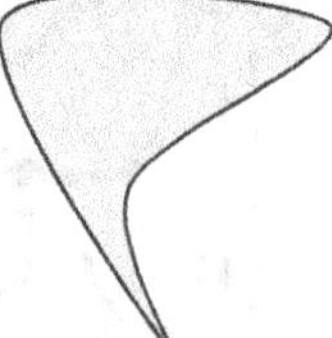

The Key To Success Is To Focus On Goals Not Obstacles

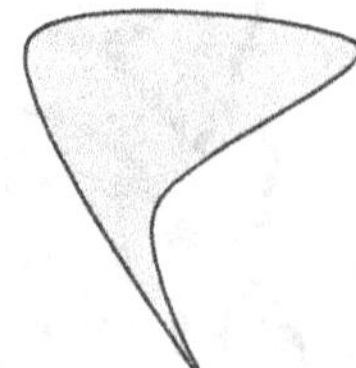

Limit Your
"Always"
And Your
"Nevers"
Amy Poehler

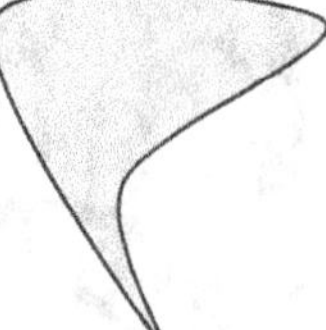

Dream It.
Wish It.
Do It.

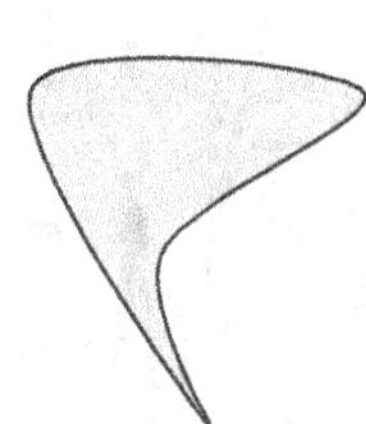

Keep Calm
& Have
Boundaries

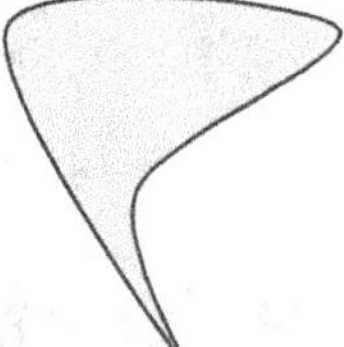

Do What
Makes
Your Soul
Shine

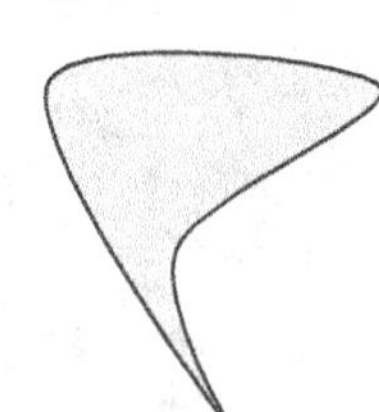

Dream It.
Wish It.
Do It.

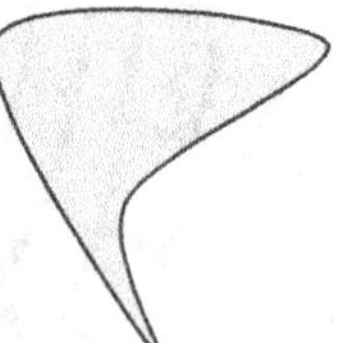

Great
Things
Rarely
Come From
Comfort
Zones

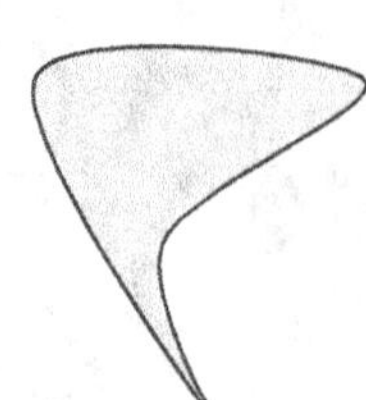

Your
Limitation—
It's Only
Your
Imagination

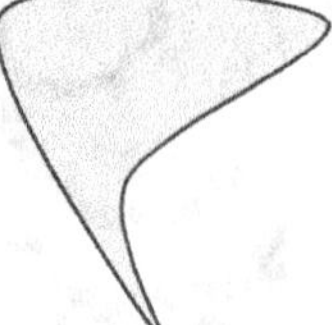

Great Things Rarely Come From Comfort Zones

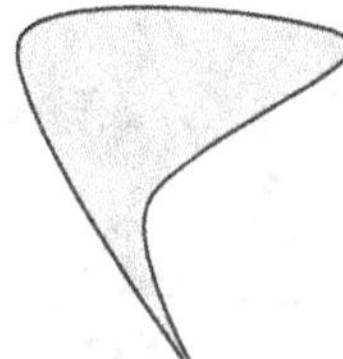

Keep Calm
& Have
Boundaries

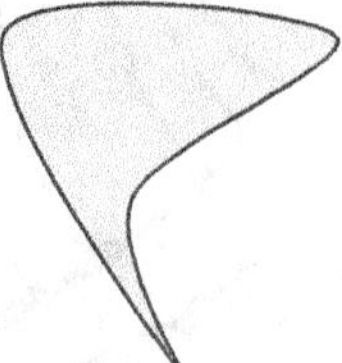

Let
Go
of the
Thoughts
That
Don't
Make
You
Strong

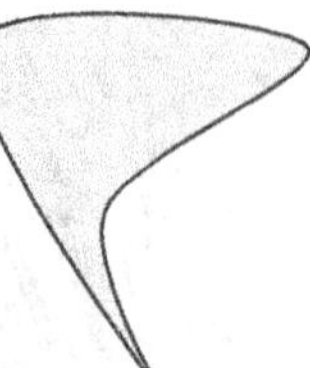

The ONLY time you should
ever look back is to see
how far you've come.

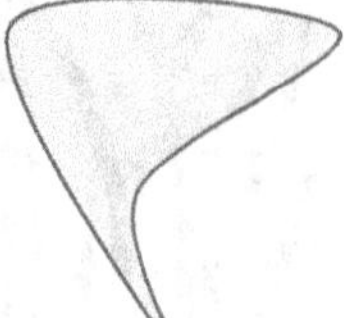

Life is short, and
it is up to you
to make it sweet. -
Sarah Louise Delany

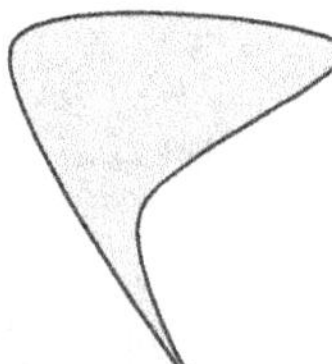

Life Is A Miracle Enjoy The Ride

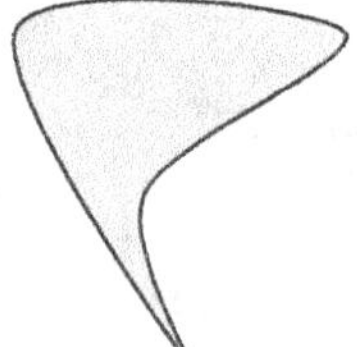

I've Got
This

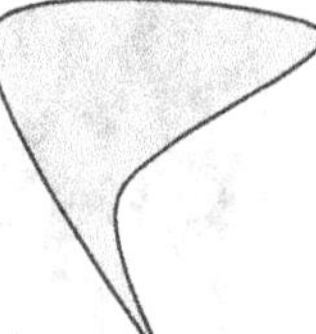

Glitter
Is Always
An Option

Escape
The
Ordinary

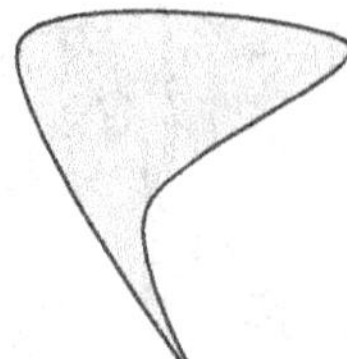

Make
Yourself
A
Priority

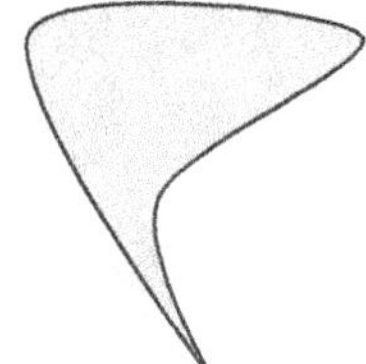

Perfectly
Imperfect

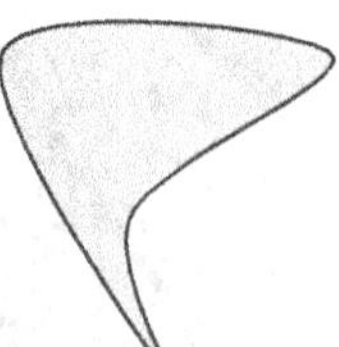

TODAY
ANYTHING IS
Possible

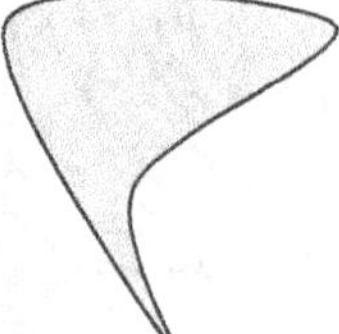

Make Your
Own
Magic

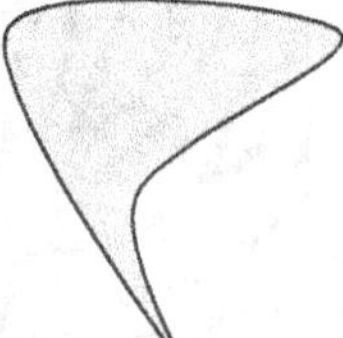

If You Know Better
Then, Do Better

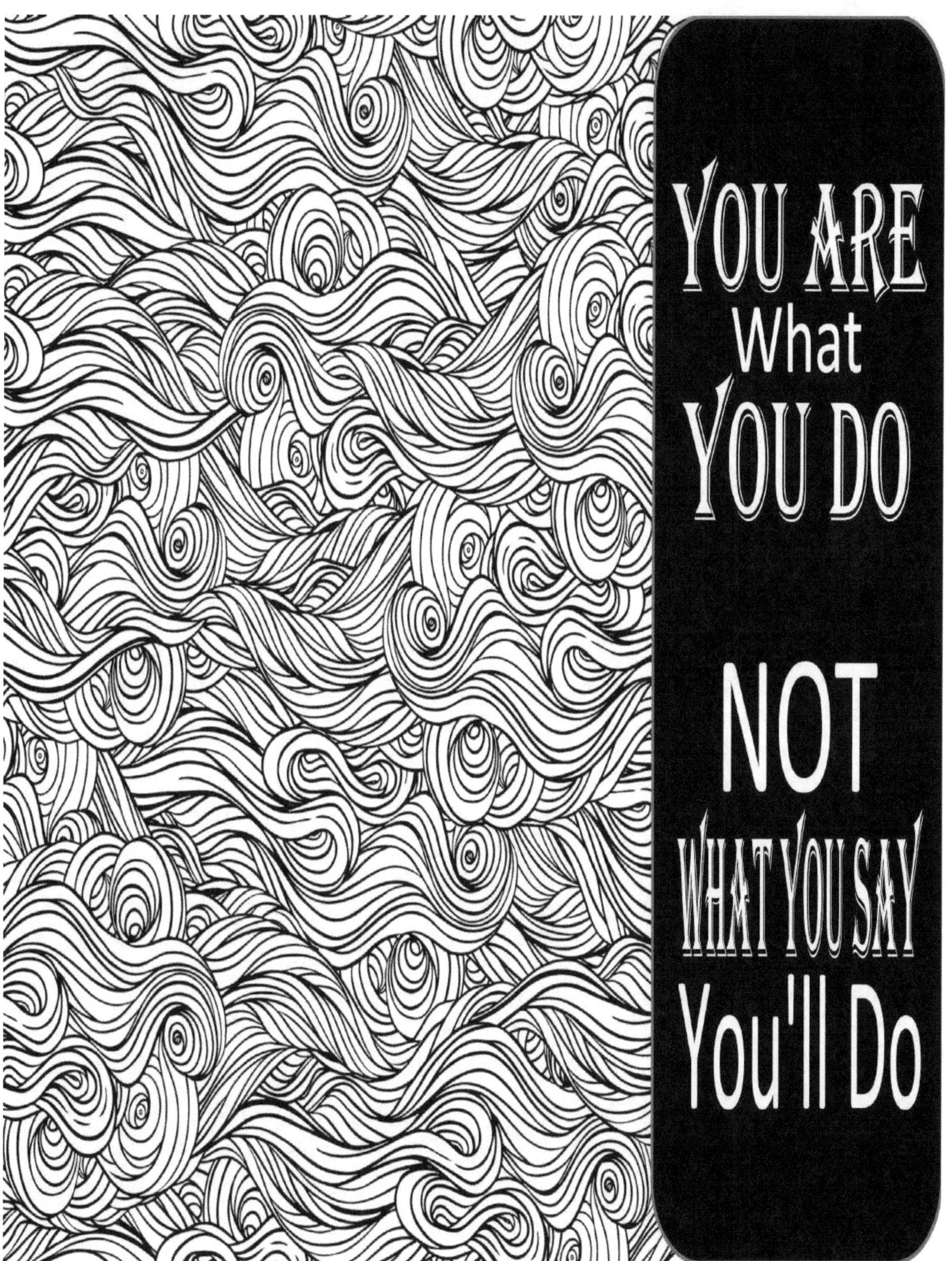

YOU ARE
What
YOU DO

NOT
WHAT YOU SAY
You'll Do

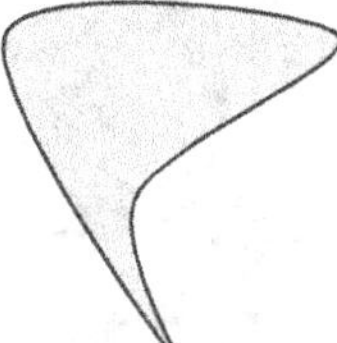

Stop
Wishing
Start
Doing

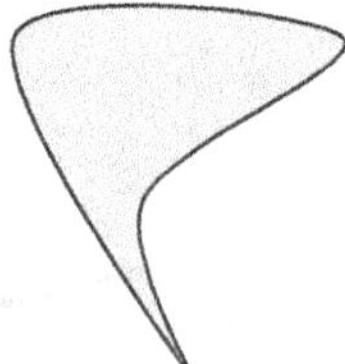

You Are
Capable
Of Amazing
Things

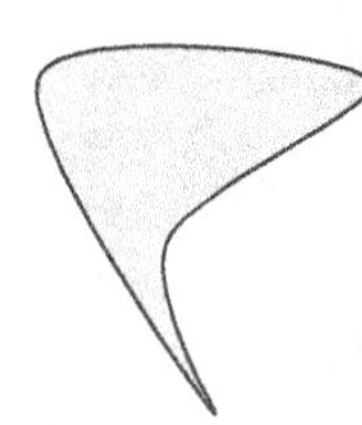

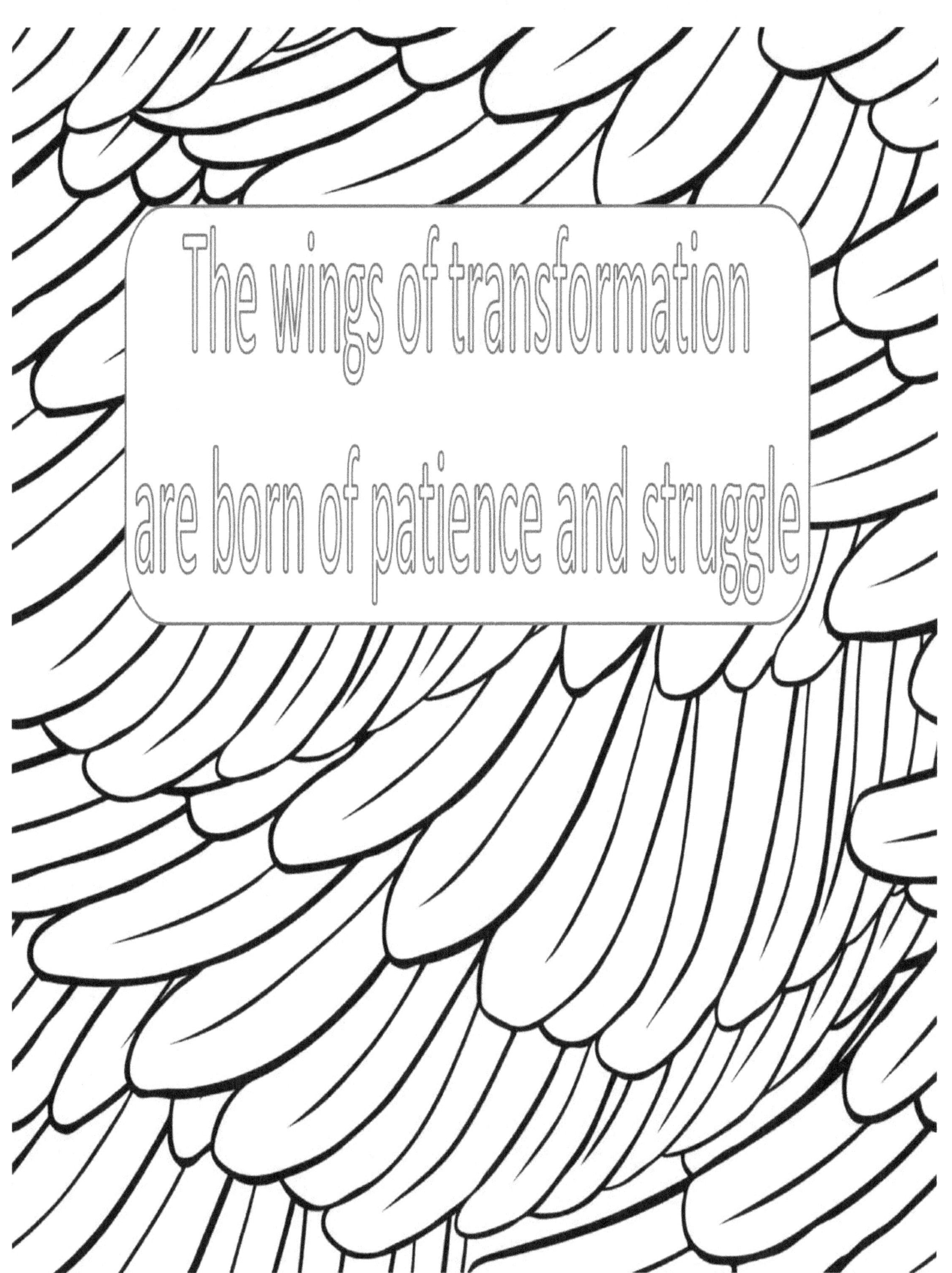
The wings of transformation
are born of patience and struggle

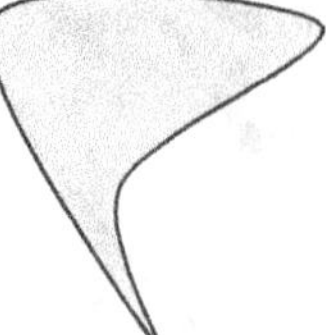

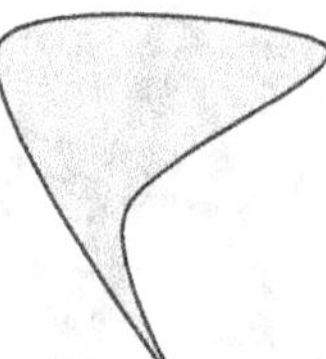

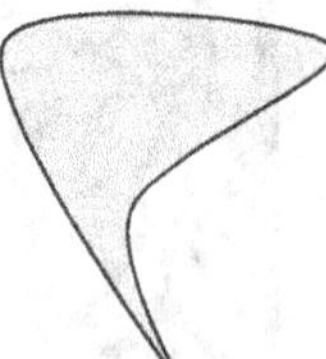

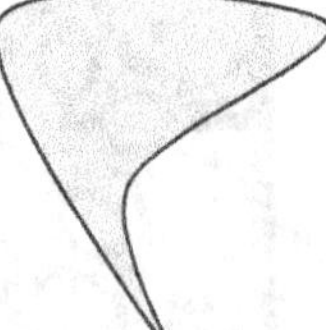

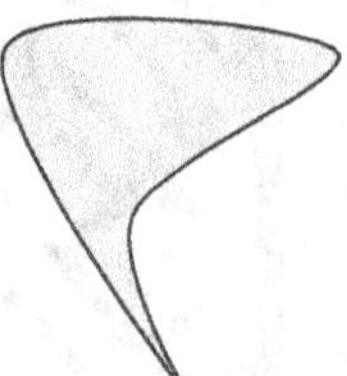

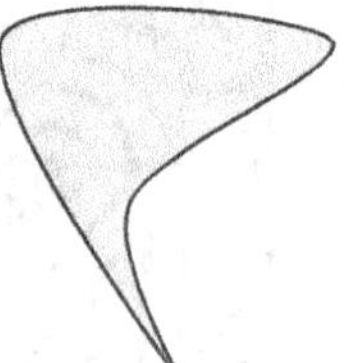

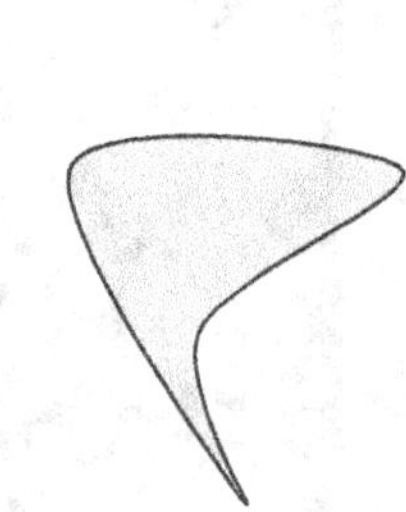

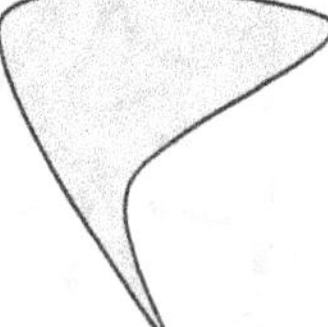

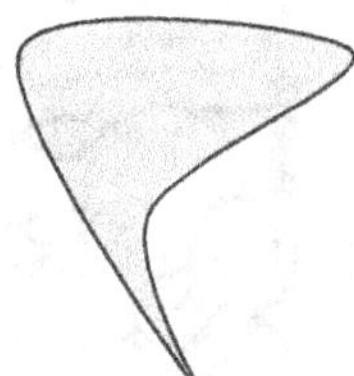

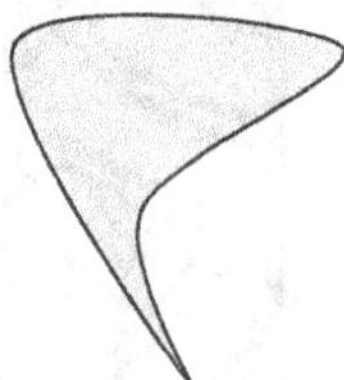

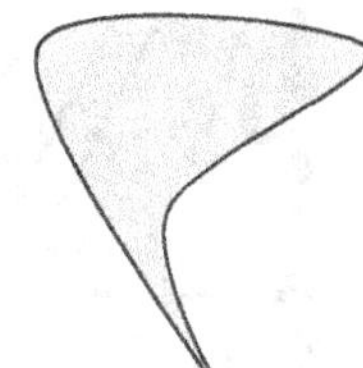

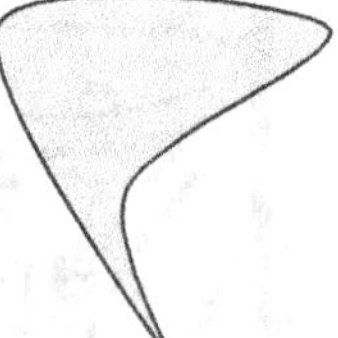

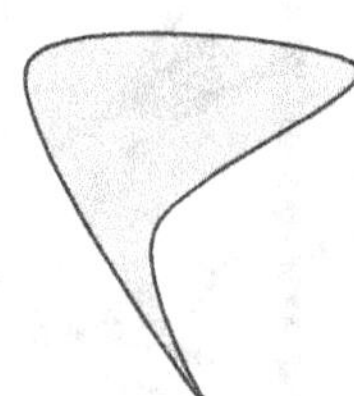

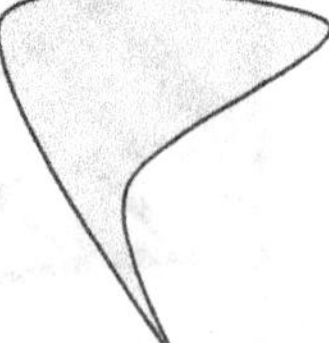

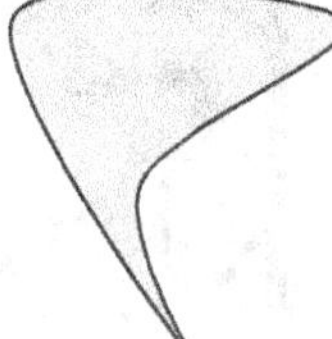

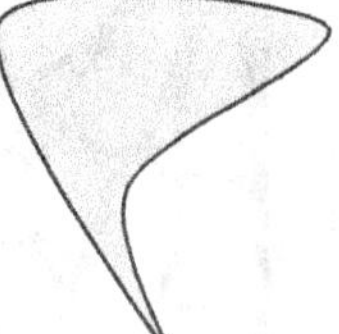

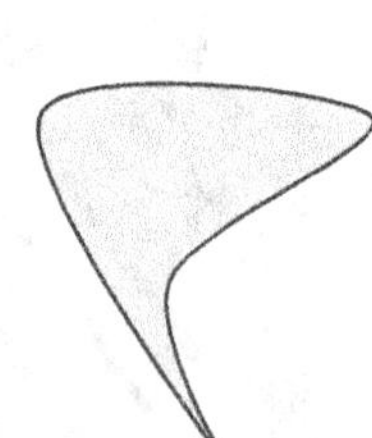

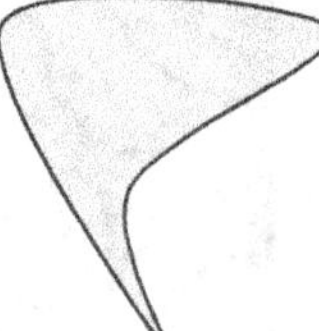